Save More

Than You Spend,

Become a Boss!

Grades 3–5

Which sounds better?

GOALS

What are those? Well, a goal is a plan or something that you want to reach and get done in the future. To reach the goal you want, you need to stick to the plan you have until you reach it. When you want the goal to happen is all up to you. It can be one month or a year; it is all up to you!

For now, I am going to keep it a little simple and show you a two-month goal. This can also be called a short-term goal.

So let us put our thinking caps on for a little bit.

One thing that I want to save money for is _____.
(This can be ANYTHING from a toy or a place you want to go. Anything.)
_____will cost $_____.
(Write whatever you are saving for.)

For me to get $_____ in two months, I will need to do a little math to see how much I will need at the end of each week.

First, take the amount you want to save and divide that by two (the two is for the two months).

Or if you have not gotten the hang of division yet, you can multiply or add using the space below. You will keep multiplying or adding two by two until you get to the amount that you want to save (which is your goal amount). You can use a separate sheet of paper if you need more space.

$_____

÷ _____

= $_____

Your total will be the amount that you will need to have each month. $_____ (per month)

WHEW! One more step to get to the amount that you will need to save each week until you reach your goal.

Since there are four weeks in each month, take the amount per month that you need to save and divide that by four.

Total per month $_____

$$\div \underline{\hspace{3cm}}$$

$$= \$\underline{\hspace{4cm}}$$

> Use this area to multiply or add instead of dividing. Keep doing 4 + 4 or 4 x 4 until you reach the amount per month to give you the amount you need to save each week.

Now I know that I will need to save $_____ each week to reach my goal, which adds up to $_____ each month.

What else do you want to save for? Maybe there is a place that you want to go to? Think big, not just thinking about toys from the store. Maybe you would like to save for:

A Disney World or Disneyland trip?
A car maybe when you get older?
Or maybe you would like to take a trip somewhere?

Save...Save...Save...

To reach a goal, we must learn how to spend less than what we save. We must force ourselves to not buy too many things that we want and spend on the things that we need. What does that mean?

That means we cannot buy something with our money every time our parents go to the store. You can get that toy next time after you reach your goal. This is called a sacrifice, giving up something to get something better and bigger! Then if you do spend, just try to save more than you spend. When we say spend on the things that you need, this means things like toothpaste, school supplies, and food and clothes (only if you don't have any). I am sure your parents take care of that for you right now, so take this time right now and thank your parents for buying you the things you need.

We will talk about how you will keep track of the money you spend later. That means you will need to know about how much you will be saving each day. To know this ahead of time before you start spending, we go back to a little math.

Go back to the amount per month $_____

÷ _____ Days in a month

= _____ Amount you should try to have each day.

Now I know all I have to do is have $_____ each day or have $_____ each week to reach my goal.

Show Me the Money!

8

Now that we know how much we should save, let us talk about the money you earn or money that is given to you. Do you do chores at home? Or how about do you have family members that give you money? Maybe they give you money for good grades or just like to give you money every time they see you. Whatever it is, wherever you get the money from, once you get it, it is yours. Now what you do with your money after you get it is up to you. Remember your goal is to get $_____.

To do that, you have to do what? SAVE MORE THAN YOU SPEND!

Below you will put down the money that you get all the time from things like chores and maybe for having good grades, or maybe just for being an awesome kid for your parents. You will do this so you can see how much money you really get and do not realize because you are usually so quick to spend it. But not anymore because we have a goal that we want to reach right? You will put the amount of money you get, where you got the money from, and when do usually get this money.

Amount	Where?	How often?

How do we make ourselves not spend as much and save more? Well, by knowing how much you need to save each time you get money before you think about spending it. For example, let us say you received $20 today for your birthday, and you know already that you need to save at least $7 each day to reach your goal. So going back to our simple math in the beginning, it's just $20 – $7 to know what you can spend. Now you would like to keep track of this to see how close you get to your goal each day, right? Well, that is what the personal balance book is for, to keep track of how you have been spending your money and to see how close you are to reaching your goals! Here is a small portion of what your balance book will look like.

Let me explain this a little bit. I know it looks like a lot, but it is not. I know you can do this; you are very smart. Your beginning amount on day one will be the amount you start with. On the next day, your beginning amount will be the amount that you ended with on the day before. Does that make sense? If you still have the money at the end of the day on one day, that means you will have that same amount of money the next day in the morning, right?

The second column is where you are going to put the amount that you need to save each day. Do you remember doing that calculation in the beginning of this book? So all you have to do is take the number from there and put it in your balance book. You will need to subtract that amount from your beginning balance.

On to the things you must buy. Remember, these are things that you really need to have like school supplies; or if you play a sport, sports equipment, things like that. Put that amount in the third column and subtract that too.

After you subtract the amount you need to save and the amount for the things that you have to buy from your beginning amount, you will now know what you have left to spend on whatever you want. You will write that amount in the fourth column. Now, if you happen to get some more money during the day, let us say from a family member that wanted to give you money or wherever you get it from, you will write that amount in the fifth column. Now at the end of the day before you go to bed, take the money you have left after you spent what you were able to spend and add it to any money you got during the day. Put that amount in the ending amount column. The ending amount is going to be your beginning amount for the next day as well, so you can go ahead and put that amount there too. Then continue to do that each day, and see how close you are getting to your goal.

I only spent $5 of my money today on something I wanted, so I did $11 - $5 = $6. Then I added the $5 I got today from recycling to the $6 I had left after spending, and that gives me $11 as my ending amount.

Day 1: Beginning amount	Amount I need to save	Amount for things I must buy	What I have left to spend	Any money I got during the day	Ending amount
$ 20	- $7	- $2	= $11	$5	=$11
Day 2: Beginning amount	Amount I need to save	Amount for things I must buy	What I have left to spend	Any money I got during the day	Amount I have at the end of the day
$	- $	- $	= $	$	=$

Now the ending amount becomes the beginning amount for the next day!

Practice on your own balance sheet here.

Day 1: Beginning amount	Amount I need to save	Amount for things I must buy	What I have left to spend	Any money I got during the day	Ending amount
$	- $	- $	= $	$	= $
Day 2: Beginning amount	Amount I need to save	Amount for things I must buy	What I have left to spend	Any money I got during the day	Amount I have at the end of the day
$	- $	- $	= $	$	= $
Day 3: Beginning amount	Amount I need to save	Amount for things I must buy	What I have left to spend	Any money I got during the day	Amount I have at the end of the day
$	- $	- $	= $	$	= $

GOAL TRACKER

Color until the line if you have completed what you needed to save for the 1st week.	Color until the line if you have completed what you needed to save for the 2nd week.	Color until the line if you have completed what you needed to save for the 3rd week.	Color until the line if you have completed what you needed to save for the 4th week.	Color until the line if you have completed what you needed to save for the 5th week.	Color until the line if you have completed what you needed to save for the 6th week.	Color until the line if you have completed what you needed to save for the 7th week.	Color until the line if you have completed what you needed to save for the 8th week.

What is your goal?

ABOUT THE AUTHOR

Athina Miles's name comes from the name Athena, who was a Greek goddess of wisdom, handicraft, and war. She thought that was very interesting because she has always been the type of person that you can easily talk to and who can give advice by sharing her wisdom. But she was also very open-minded and okay with learning from others as well. Besides being an ear to others, she has enjoyed and loved playing basketball since she was a little girl. She has played for the YMCA, AAU, and all four years of high school.

She was born and raised in Stockton, California and was the oldest of six children. Being the oldest can be a little tough because you have the weight of the little ones looking up to you. So that is what she has strived to do—be the best to show them that you can achieve anything that you put your mind to.

Her last year of high school had an accounting class, and that's where she realized she was really good with numbers. She graduated high school and went to get her degree in accounting. She then started working in the accounting field. That is the best job—a job that she loves to do not just because she needed the money. Remember that.

She has traveled, vacationed, moved out of state then came back home, so she has been enjoying life. She has two children, and her son is the oldest. As she keeps telling him, "Save your money, save your money." She realized she had to show him. She did a practice run of this book with him. Then it dawned on her that she wished she had this when she was growing up. She would have been doing what she is doing now at an early age. God placed her in the accounting field for a reason, and she believes part of that reason is this book, besides the fact that her kids inspire her to do the best she can for them. This book is not for the money, but for the future of the youth and to brighten their mind to think bigger and wiser.